SAND BOTTOMS

By Melissa Cole

Photographs By Brandon Cole

BLACKBIRCH®
PRESS

THOMSON
★
GALE ™

San Diego • Detroit • New York • San Francisco • Cleveland • New Haven, Conn. • Waterville, Maine • London • Munich

For more information, contact
The Gale Group, Inc.
27500 Drake Rd.
Farmington Hills, MI 48331-3535
Or you can visit our Internet site at http://www.gale.com

Photo Credits: Cover, all photos © Brandon D. Cole; illustrations by Chris Jouan Illustration

LIBRARY OF CONGRESS CATALOGING-IN-PUBLICATION DATA

Cole, Melissa S.
 Sand bottoms / by Melissa S. Cole.
  v. cm. — (Wild marine habitats)
Includes bibliographical references (p.).
Contents: Where are sand bottoms found today? — Climate — Plants — Animals.
 ISBN 1-56711-910-7 (hardback : alk. paper)
 1. Sublittoral ecology—Juvenile literature. [1. Coastal ecology. 2. Ecology.] I. Title II.
Series: Cole, Melissa S. Wild marine habitats.

 QH541.5.S87C65 2004
 577.7'8—dc22   2003019615

Contents

Introduction

A habitat is a place where certain plants and animals are found living together naturally. There are many different habitats beneath the surface of the world's oceans. One of these ocean habitats is the sand bottom. Sand bottoms are formed when rain washes sand, mud, or volcanic ash into the ocean. This creates large sandy areas of seafloor that look like underwater deserts. Sand bottoms are also found near the mouths of rivers. There, muddy water pours into the ocean. Particles of sand and dirt mixed with river water enter the ocean and sink to the bottom. They form sandy bays called estuaries, where fresh river water mixes with salty seawater.

Sharks and other large predators often swim over sand bottoms, the large sandy areas of the seafloor that look like underwater deserts, in search of food.

Sand bottoms are found worldwide in coastal waters. The sand bottoms with the largest variety of living creatures are found in the Caribbean, the Indo-Pacific, and the West Coast of North America. Sand bottoms stretch from the shoreline where the waves break, to the edge of the continental shelf. The continental shelf is the sandy ocean floor that runs from the edge of a continent to the continental slope, where the water gets very deep. Sand bottoms can be found in water as deep as 140 feet (43 m).

Sand bottoms start where the waves break at the shoreline (pictured) and reach to the edge of the continental shelf.

What Makes Sand Bottoms Unique?

Sand bottoms are difficult places for plants and animals to live in because waves and currents keep the sand constantly in motion. Very few plants can settle and grow in the shifting sands. Sand bottoms do not offer animals many places to hide from predators. When animals hide in the sand, they may be covered one minute and exposed the next.

Storms, currents, and waves keep the sand moving all the time so animals cannot hide from predators.

Sand bottoms are found in many different climates. Some are in near-freezing Arctic oceans. Some are in warm tropical seas near coastal coral reefs. Sand bottom habitats are greatly affected by storms. Storms bring strong winds, pounding waves, and fast currents. These forces stir up the sand bottom and wash away living creatures.

Colorful wildlife lives on the sand bottoms of tropical seas while tougher creatures (inset) inhabit those of the near-freezing Arctic.

Only a few types of plants are able to live in the shifting sands along the bottom. Eelgrass is the most common plant found on sand bottoms. With its long, thin shape, it resembles an eel. It grows most often in estuaries near river mouths. Eelgrass is important because it provides food and a place to hide for many sand bottom animals.

Another type of plant, algae, grows in both warm and cool water. It is found in deeper waters that range from 80 to 140 feet (24 to 43 m) below the surface. In deep water, the sand bottom is less affected by waves and currents and does not shift as much. This calmer water allows a layer of algae to coat the sand.

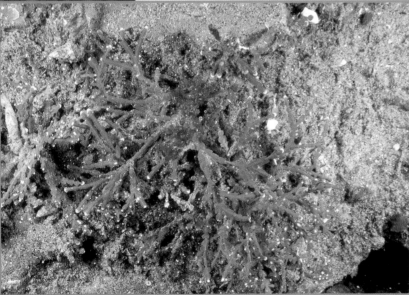

Because the sand constantly shifts, only a few plants like eelgrass (opposite) and algae (inset) are able to live along the bottom.

11

Many large predators visit the sand bottom habitat to hunt the smaller animals that live there. In warm water, nurse sharks and hammerheads often swim over sand bottoms in search of food. They can sense the weak electrical signals given off by their prey's muscles. Sharks can even use this sense to find fish, crabs, and sea snails that are buried beneath the sand.

Dolphins also visit sand bottoms to feed. They use a radarlike sense called echolocation to find prey such as razorfish. Once dolphins locate a fish, they use their long snouts to dig the prey out from beneath the sand.

Dolphins use their long snouts to dig out prey that is buried in the sand.

Gray whales visit Arctic sand bottoms to find food. Instead of teeth, they have long hairy pieces of baleen. Baleen plates are like stiff bristle brushes that hang from a whale's top jaw. Gray whales use this baleen to strain animals such as crabs, worms, and shellfish from the muddy bottom.

The gray whale's baleen plate (pictured) strains small sea creatures from the sand on the ocean floor.

Sand bottoms are also home to smaller predators such as rays, flounder, and stargazers. All of these animals have flat bodies whose color blends in with the sand. Many of these animals bury their bodies beneath the sand with only their eyeballs sticking out. This helps them hide from enemies and hunt prey at the same time. When a fish swims over them, they lunge out of the sand and gulp down their food in an instant.

Some fish hide in the sand with only their eyeballs sticking out so that they can remain safe from predators while they hunt their own prey.

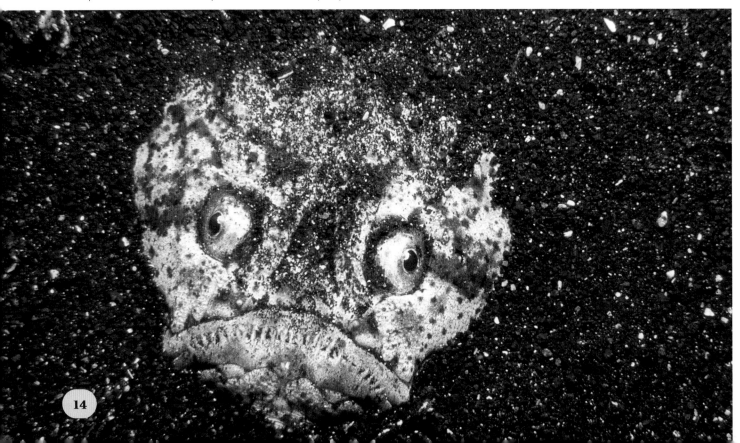

Fish such as halibut, flounder, and sand dabs are known as flatfish. Flatfish begin life like most other fish, with their eyes on either side of their head. They swim upright through the water, and their tails move from side to side. As they grow into adults, however, one of their eyes moves to the opposite side of the head, near the other eye. The side with both eyes then becomes the top of the fish. The other side of the body becomes the bottom.

Flatfish like flounder and halibut rest right on the sand bottom.

The adult flatfish swims along the sandy bottom with its tail moving up and down like a stingray. When adult flatfish rest, one side of their body rests flat against the sand bottom. Both eyes look upward from the other side of their body.

Other tropical sand bottom predators use camouflage to avoid being eaten by larger predators. For example, cockatoo waspfish, hairy frogfish, and double-ended pipefish look like dead leaves, algae, and eelgrass. The mimic octopus imitates the behavior and appearance of crabs, jellyfish, or sea snakes to avoid being eaten. Predators usually try to avoid these dangerous animals because of their claws, stinging tentacles, and poisonous fangs. When the mimic octopus imitates a jellyfish, it lets its arms hang below it like jellyfish tentacles. As a crab it forms a ball and scuttles along the bottom with a crablike motion. It even curls its front arms to look like claws. When it acts like a sea snake, it buries itself below the sand except for two arms, which it waves to look like snakes.

Camouflage allows some fish to blend into the sand (above) while others look like the plants (below) on the sand bottom.

Some sand bottom animals use a poison called venom to keep their enemies away. The stingray has a venomous barb on the end of its tail that it can use to sting predators when attacked. The giant nudibranch, a type of sea slug that lives in cool water, steals stinging cells from its prey. These nudibranchs eat the tentacles of tube anemones, which are full of stinging cells. Giant nudibranchs can swallow these cells without digesting them. The nudibranchs pass the stinging cells to their own feathery gills, where they serve as protection from predators.

A few animals work together to avoid being eaten. For example, a small fish called a goby forms a partnership with a blind shrimp. The shrimp builds a burrow of sand and mud, keeps it clean, and shares it with the goby. Since the shrimp is unable to see, it is the goby's job to guard the entrance to the burrow and watch for enemies. When predators approach, the goby flicks its tail to warn the shrimp. Together, they dart deep into the burrow to hide.

The nudibranch (above) protects itself with its stinging cells, but gobies and shrimp (below) just hide in burrows.

Many sand bottom animals are known as filter feeders. They strain the tiny plants and animals known as plankton from the water. Filter feeders use a variety of methods to trap plankton that drifts by. For example, tubeworms extend a crown of feathery gills from their tube opening to catch bits of plankton.

Clams and scallops are also filter feeders. To feed, buried clams use two tubes called siphons that they extend out of their shells and up through the sand. One siphon filters plankton from the water and the other siphon carries wastewater away. These animals are especially plentiful in cool sand bottom areas.

Tubeworms (above), clams, and scallops (below) are filter feeders that strain plankton from the water.

Garden eels also feed on plankton. They live together in large colonies and are found on sand bottoms in tropical waters worldwide. Each garden eel has an individual burrow below the sand. During the day they raise their heads and long bodies from their burrows to pick small pieces of plankton from the water. When danger approaches, they sink back down into their burrows and hide.

Some sand bottom animals graze on the layer of algae that grows on top of the sand. Olive snails are grazers found on tropical sand bottoms. They crawl on a muscular organ called a foot. Olive snails have a rough tongue that they use to scrape algae off the bottom.

Garden eels emerge from their burrows to eat plankton.

Sand dollars, which are related to starfish and sea urchins, also feed on algae. They crawl along the bottom using hundreds of tube feet. Tube feet are tiny, water-filled tubes with suction cups on the ends. When enemies or storms approach, sand dollars are able to bury themselves quickly with their tube feet.

Sand bottoms are kept clean by a group of animals known as scavengers. For example, shrimp, hermit crabs, and brittle starfish feed on dead plants and animals that settle on the sand bottom. Animals such as worms and sea cucumbers sift through the sand and eat any scraps that remain. Many of these animals are found in both warm and cool waters.

Sand dollars use their tiny tube feet to quickly bury themselves in the sand.

A Sand Bottom's Food Chain

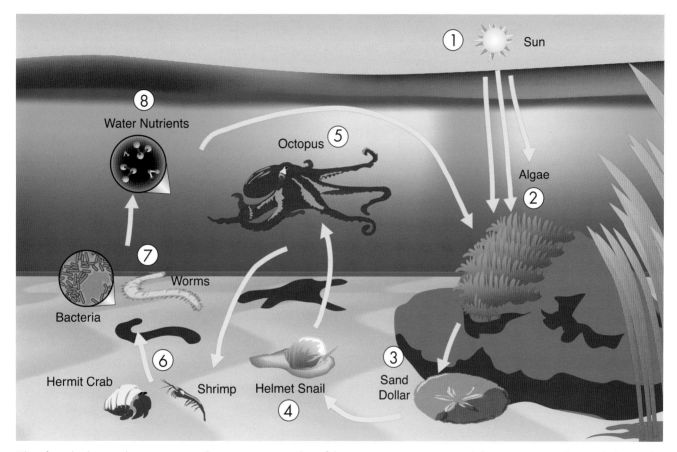

The food chain shows a step-by-step example of how energy in a sand bottom is exchangd through food: (1) sunlight is used by (2) algae to make sugar. When a (3) sand dollar eats the algae, some of the plant's energy becomes part of the sand dollar. When a (4) helmet snail eats the sand dollar, and when a larger predator such as an (5) octopus eats the helmet snail, the energy is passed on from creature to creature. When the octopus dies, scavengers such as (6) shrimp and hermit crabs feed on the waste. Decomposers such as (7) worms and bacteria break down the last bits until they become part of the sand or mix with the seawater. Algae absorbs these (8) nutrients directly from the water in addition to the energy it receives from the sun. Then the whole cycle begins again.

Humans and Sand Bottoms

Pollution along the shoreline damages sand bottoms and harms the many animals that live there.

Sand bottoms are easily damaged by pollution. When it rains, pollutants run into the ocean. They then sink to the bottom and mix with the sand. When animals feed on algae and food particles, these pollutants enter their bodies. Eventually, this can make people sick when they eat seafood.

The way people collect wild shrimp damages sand bottoms. They drag heavy nets across the sand that capture everything in their way. They also dig up the bottom.

To help prevent these problems, people can join conservation groups. People can also limit the amount of wild shrimp they eat. These actions should help sand bottom habitats remain healthy in the future.

A Sand Bottom's Food Web

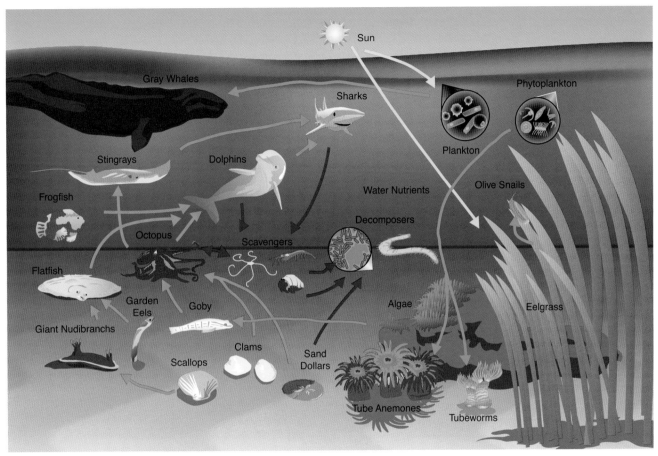

Food webs show how creatures in a habitat depend on one another to survive. The arrows in this drawing show the flow of energy from one creature to another. Yellow arrows: green plants that make food from water and sunlight; green arrows: animals that eat the green plants; orange arrows: predators; red arrows: scavengers and decomposers. These reduce dead bodies to their basic chemicals, which return to the soil to be taken up by green plants, beginning the cycle all over again.

Glossary

Algae Simple plants that do not produce roots or flowers

Camouflage A coloration, shape, or behavior that allows a plant or animal to be hidden or disguised in its environment

Decomposers Animals such as worms and bacteria that eat dead tissue and return nutrients to the water

Echolocation A special ability that dolphins have. They send out sound waves to create a sound picture of prey hidden beneath the sand. It is similar to radar used by bats.

Habitat The place in which a plant or animal naturally lives. Habitats normally provide living organisms with everything they need to survive-food, water, and shelter.

Predators Animals that hunt other animals for food

Prey An animal hunted by another animal

Scavengers Animals such as starfish that feed on dead animals

Venom A poison that some animals use for hunting and self-defense

For More Information

Books

Cohat, Elizabeth. *The Seashore*. New York: Scholastic, 1995.

Feltner, Patricia K., *Brittle Stars and Mudbugs*. Seattle: Sasquatch Books, 2001.

McLeish, Ewan. *Habitats: Oceans and Seas*. Austin, TX: Steck-Vaughn, 1997.

Web site

This Monterey Bay Aquarium site describes sand bottom habitats.

www.mbayaq.org/cr/cr_seafoodwatch/sfw_hd.asp

Index